To:

You are **unstoppable,**

**unbreakable** and **unshakeable,**

only with God.

Minister Rich P. Successful

Date

1975

DIVES

VALDE · FELIX

PROSPERUM

S

Fidem   Remissionem   Humilitas

# Dedication

To my beloved kids, my wife, family, and future generations,

There were moments when giving up seemed like the easier path. But imagine if I had succumbed to those challenges—if I had let them define me. You wouldn't have this prayer journal in your hands today, guiding you through pitfalls and turning them into pit stops—a place for refueling and rejuvenation. Certainly, you might not fully grasp the profound truth that with God, we are all unstoppable, unbreakable, and unshakeable.

This journal is not just a book; it's a testament, a living testimony to the faithfulness of God. Through the trials and tribulations, I faced, God's strength shone through, showing that my troubles did not define me, but rather defined the greatness of the God I serve.

Let this journey inspire you. Embrace the legacy of resilience and faith, knowing that your strength is rooted in something far greater than the challenges you face. With God by your side, no obstacle is insurmountable. May you carry this truth with you, shaping your path and leaving a legacy of hope and empowerment for generations to come.

With all my love and empowerment,

Rich P. Successful

# Introduction

Welcome to this prayer journal, a testament to the limitless possibilities of what God will do when you place your trust in Him. As you journey through the chapters focusing on being Unstoppable, Unbreakable, and Unshakeable, remember that your better days are not behind you; they are still ahead. God has a unique and powerful purpose for your life that is unfolding with each moment.

Embrace this truth: every second counts in the eyes of God. Each moment holds the potential for transformation, healing, and growth. As you engage with each day in this journal, I encourage you to make every second count. Life is fleeting, and it is often in the small, seemingly insignificant moments that God works His greatest miracles.

This journal is designed to be your constant companion, easily traveling with you wherever you go. Whether you're at the barber shop, beauty salon, on a flight, waiting in a coffee shop, or during a commute, it is crafted to fit seamlessly into your day, providing you with the opportunity to continually renew your mind with the truth of God's word. Its portability ensures that you can keep your focus on God's promises, no matter where life takes you.

Rather than examining your life purely through the lens of your own understanding and circumstances, shift your perspective to see what your life means to God. Your experiences, trials, and triumphs are each vital components of His grand design. Let this journal be your guide as you navigate the challenges ahead and uncover the extraordinary power of a life anchored in faith.

May this journal inspire you to step boldly into the future, fortified by the knowledge that with God, nothing is impossible. Embrace the journey, and know that you are embarking on a destiny-altering path toward true spiritual empowerment.

With Faith,

Rich P. Successful

Dear Friends,

We are thrilled to share this prayer journal with you as a gift, and we invite you to help us expand our reach by sowing a seed into our ministry. Your seed gift empowers our mission, making it possible for us to share this powerful tool with others at no cost—whether at the gas station, grocery store, community center, or during local events.

Your generosity allows us to provide these journals to those in need, ensuring that God's love and truth reach as many hearts as possible. We trust that God will bless your support, enriching your life as you help us impact the world.

If you feel led to give, please consider making your gift via Cash App. We've attached our Cash App barcode for your convenience.

Thank you for your prayers and commitment to this divine mission.

With gratitude,

Rich P. Successful

# Table of Contents

# Unstoppable

## Day 1:

### You are Unstoppable!
**Scripture:** Matthew 14:29

**Reflection:** Consider Peter's courage to step out of doubt and onto the water.

**Prayer Prompt:** Ask God for the courage to step out of doubt, into faith and trust Him unwavering.

**Questions**:


What 'boat' of doubt can you step out of to become unstoppable in your faith walk?

_____

_____

_____

_____

How would trusting God more fully make you unstoppable in your daily life?

_____

_____

_____

_____

Who inspires you to live courageously and be unstoppable in your commitments?

_____

_____

_____

_____

What steps can you take today to move toward being unstoppable in your walk with God?

_____

_____

_____

_____

## Day 2:

**Uncompromising Faith!**
**Scripture:** 1 Samuel 2:25

**Reflection**: Reflect on the dangers of compromising your faith.

**Prayer Prompt**: Pray for discernment and strength to eliminate compromise.

**Questions:**

What areas of your life need to be uncompromised to stay unstoppable?

_____

_____

_____

_____

How has compromise hindered your ability to be an unstoppable force for God?

_____

_____

_____

_____

What specific compromises can you eliminate to better align with God's will?

_____

_____

_____

_____

How does being unstoppable in your faith influence others around you?

_____

_____

_____

_____

## Day 3:

### Rebuilding Foundations of Faith!
**Scripture:** Psalm 127:1

**Reflection**: Think about areas in your life where foundations of faith need to be rebuilt on Christ.

**Prayer Prompt:** Ask God to help rebuild your life on His principles.

**Questions**:

What foundations of faith in your life need to be rebuilt to become unstoppable?

_____

_____

_____

_____

How can rebuilding your foundation on Christ make you unbreakable in your faith?

_____

_____

_____

_____

Which principles of Christ do you need to focus on to strengthen your foundation of faith?

_____

_____

_____

_____

What actions can you take today to start rebuilding your faith foundation?

_____

_____

_____

_____

## Day 4:

### God's Plan!
### Scripture: Jeremiah 29:11

**Reflection:** Trust that God has a plan for delay, prosperity and hope.

**Prayer Prompt:** Pray for patience and trust in God's plan for your life.

**Questions:**

How does trusting in God's plan help you remain unshakeable in the face of delay?

_____

_____

_____

_____

What aspects of God's plan are you struggling to trust Him with?

_____

_____

_____

_____

In what ways can trusting God's plan make you unstoppable in your pursuits?

_____

_____

_____

_____

How can you remind yourself in the delay of God's promise of a hopeful outcome?

_____

_____

_____

_____

## Day 5:

### Overcoming the Vulture Culture!
**Scripture**: Romans 12:2

**Reflection**: Consider how societal norms and behaviors prey on your relationship with God.

**Prayer Prompt:** Ask for transformation and renewal of your mind from the culture to focus on God.

**Questions:**

How can you transform your mind to become unshakeable against vulture cultures (worldly influences)?

_____

_____

_____

_____

What vulture cultures do you need to overcome
to stay unstoppable in your faith?

_____

_____

_____

_____

What practical steps can you take to renew your
mind according to God's will for your life?

_____

_____

_____

_____

How does overcoming vulture culture empower
you to fulfill your divine purpose?

_____

_____

_____

_____

## Day 6:

### Strength against Challenges!
### Scripture: Romans 8:28

**Reflection**: Remember that God works all things for his good for you.

**Prayer Prompt**: Pray for strength to endure and overcome life's giants (challenges).

**Questions:**

How can you remind yourself that challenges are opportunities to become unbreakable?

_____

_____

_____

_____

In what ways does facing challenges head-on make you unstoppable?

_____

_____

_____

_____

How has God worked in the past challenges for good in your life?

_____

_____

_____

_____

What challenges are you currently facing that require God's strength to overcome?

_____

_____

_____

_____

## Day 7:

### Spiritual Leadership!
**Scripture:** Joshua 24:15

**Reflection**: Reflect on Joshua's commitment to lead his household in serving the Lord.

**Prayer Prompt**: Pray for godly leadership in your home and community.

**Questions:**

How can being a spiritual leader make you unshakeable in your household?

_____

_____

_____

_____

What qualities of Joshua's leadership do you admire and wish to emulate in your household?

_____

_____

_____

_____

In what ways can you lead by example to inspire your household to be unstoppable?

_____

_____

_____

_____

How does committing to serve the Lord strengthen your role as a spiritual leader?

_____

_____

_____

_____

## Day 8:

### Helping Others Stand!
**Scripture:** Galatians 6:2

**Reflection**: Think about how you can help others bear their burdens.

**Prayer Prompt**: Pray for opportunities to support and uplift others in faith.

**Questions:**

How can helping others with their burdens make you unshakeable in your community?

_____

_____

_____

_____

What specific ways can you support someone today to help them become unstoppable?

_____

_____

_____

_____

How does bearing one another's burdens fulfill the love of Christ in your life?

_____

_____

_____

_____

Who in your life can you reach out to and offer support and encouragement?

_____

_____

_____

_____

## Day 9:

### Embracing Your Stolen Identity!
### Scripture: Genesis 1:27

**Reflection:** Reflect on being made in God's image, likeness, presence and power.

**Prayer Prompt:** Pray to embrace your stolen (divine) identity and purpose.

**Questions:**

How can embracing your stolen identity in Christ make you unbreakable in faith?

_____

_____

_____

_____

According to John 10:10 in what ways has your true identity (Genesis 1:27) in God been stolen.

_____

_____

_____

_____

How does knowing you are made in God's image empower you to be unstoppable?

_____

_____

_____

_____

What steps can you take to live more fully in your God-given identity today?

_____

_____

_____

_____

# Day 10:

## Live Like You Never Been Hurt!
### Scripture: Psalm 147:3

**Reflection**: Contemplate God's power to heal broken hearts.

**Prayer Prompt**: Ask God for healing from past wounds and traumas.

**Questions**:

How can living like you never been hurt offer healing from past hurts make you unbreakable in your journey forward?

_____

_____

_____

_____

What past hurts are currently delaying your ability to live an unstoppable life?

_____

_____

_____

_____

How has God's healing power been evident in your life?

_____

_____

_____

_____

What steps can you take now to seek God's healing and move past your traumas?

_____

_____

_____

_____

# Day 11:

## Resisting Temptational Reset!
### Scripture: 1 Corinthians 10:13

**Reflection**: Remember that God provides a way out of every temptation.

**Prayer Prompt:** Pray for strength to resist temptations that cause you to reset (go back to the end of God's line of blessing) and stand firm in faith.

**Questions**:


How does resisting temptation make your faith unbreakable?

_____

_____

_____

_____

What temptations are you currently struggling with that hinder your unstoppable journey?

_____

_____

_____

_____

How can you rely on God's provision to escape temptational reset?

_____

_____

_____

_____

What practical measures can you implement to resist and overcome temptational reset?

_____

_____

_____

_____

# Day 12:

## Godly Unity in Relationships!
**Scripture:** Ephesians 4:3

**Reflection:** Consider the importance of Godly unity in your household and family.

**Prayer Prompt:** Pray for reconciliation and Godly unity in all your relationships.

**Questions:**

How can fostering Godly unity in your relationships make you unbreakable as a community?

_____

_____

_____

_____

What relationships need healing and God's unity to make your journey unstoppable?

_____

_____

_____

_____

How can you actively promote Godly unity within your family and church?

_____

_____

_____

_____

What role does forgiveness play in achieving unshakeable Godly unity?

_____

_____

_____

_____

## Day 13:

### Strength in Adversity!
**Scripture:** Philippians 4:13

**Reflection:** Meditate on Paul's declaration of strength through Christ.

**Prayer Prompt:** Pray for strength and perseverance in difficult times.

**Questions:**

How can Christ's strength make you unbreakable in times of adversity?

_____

_____

_____

_____

What adversities are you currently facing that challenge your faith?

_____

_____

_____

_____

How does relying on Christ's strength help you remain unstoppable?

_____

_____

_____

_____

What are some practical ways to draw on Christ's strength daily?

_____

_____

_____

_____

## Day 14:

### Overcoming The Spirit of Fear!
**Scripture**: 2 Timothy 1:7

**Reflection:** Reflect on God's gift of faith, power, love, and a sound mind.

**Prayer Prompt:** Pray for deliverance from all fears, anxieties and depression.

**Questions:**

How can embracing God's power help you become unshakeable against fear?

_____

_____

_____

_____

What fears are holding you back from being
unstoppable in your faith and life?

_____

_____

_____

_____

How does knowing God has given you a spirit of
faith empower you to overcome fear?

_____

_____

_____

_____

What steps can you take today to conquer your
fears with God's help?

_____

_____

_____

_____

## Day 15:

### God Will Sustain You!
**Scripture:** Psalm 55:22

**Reflection**: Trust in God to sustain you through all challenges.

**Prayer Prompt**: Pray for God's sustaining power in your life.

**Questions:**

How does trusting in God's sustenance help you remain unbreakable?

_____

_____

_____

_____

What challenges do you need God's sustaining
power to overcome?

_____

_____

_____

_____

• How has God sustained you through difficult
times in the past?

_____

_____

_____

_____

• What daily practices can help you rely more
on God's sustenance?

_____

_____

_____

_____

## Day 16:

### Living With Integrity In The Ups and Downs!
### Scripture: Proverbs 10:9

**Reflection**: Consider the importance of walking in integrity.

**Prayer Prompt:** Pray for the strength to live a life of integrity.

**Questions**:

How can living with integrity make you unstoppable in your Christian walk?

_____

_____

_____

_____

What areas of your life need more integrity to become unbreakable?

_____

_____

_____

_____

How does integrity influence how others perceive your faith?

_____

_____

_____

_____

What actions can you take to ensure you are walking in integrity daily?

_____

_____

_____

_____

## Day 17:

### Commitment to Truth!
### Scripture: John 8:32

**Reflection**: Meditate on the freedom found in God's truth.

**Prayer Prompt**: Pray for a deep commitment to living in God's truth.

**Questions**:

How can a commitment to truth make you unshakeable in your convictions?

_____

_____

_____

_____

What truths of God need to be more prevalent in your everyday life to be unstoppable?

_____

_____

_____

_____

How has knowing the truth set you free in the past?

_____

_____

_____

_____

What practices can help you stay committed to living out God's truth?

_____

_____

_____

_____

## Unshakeable

## Day 18:

### Unshakeable Faith!
**Scripture:** Hebrews 12:28

**Reflection**: Reflect on receiving an unshakeable kingdom.

**Prayer Prompt:** Pray for unshakeable faith and trust in God.

**Questions**:

How does understanding you belong to an unshakeable kingdom inspire your faith?

_____

_____

_____

_____

In what areas do you want to develop unshakeable faith?

_____

_____

_____

_____

How can unshakeable faith make you unstoppable in achieving your God-given goals?

_____

_____

_____

_____

What practical steps can you take to build and sustain unshakeable faith?

_____

_____

_____

_____

# Day 19:

## Standing Firm In The Delays!
## Scripture: James 1:12

**Reflection**: Consider the blessing of enduring delays through faith.

**Prayer Prompt:** Pray for steadfastness in the face of delays.

**Questions**:

How can enduring delays build an unshakeable character in you?

_____

_____

_____

_____

What current delays are testing your ability to remain steadfast and unbreakable?

_____

_____

_____

_____

How does standing firm in delays make you unstoppable in your journey with God?

_____

_____

_____

_____

What biblical examples can you draw from to inspire perseverance in delays?

_____

_____

_____

_____

## Day 20:

### Victory over the Faithlessness!
**Scripture:** Ephesians 6:11

**Reflection**: Reflect on the importance of God's armor in spiritual warfare.

**Prayer Prompt:** Pray for strength and protection against spiritual attacks.

**Questions**:

How can putting on the full armor of God help you remain unshakeable in spiritual warfare?

_____

_____

_____

_____

What spiritual battles are you currently facing that hinder your unstoppable progress?

_____

_____

_____

_____

How has God equipped you for victory over the enemy of faithlessness?

_____

_____

_____

_____

What daily practices can help you stay prepared for spiritual attacks against your faith in God?

_____

_____

_____

_____

## Day 21:

**God's Inexhaustible Love!**
**Scripture**: Romans 8:38-39

**Reflection**: Meditate on the unshakeable love of God.

**Prayer Prompt:** Pray to experience and share the depth of God's love.

**Questions:**

How can experiencing God's everlasting love make you unshakeable in your faith?

_____

_____

_____

_____

What barriers prevent you from fully embracing
God's unshakeable love?

_____

_____

_____

_____

How does God's love empower you to be
unstoppable in loving others?

_____

_____

_____

_____

What actions can you take to share God's love
more effectively in your community?

_____

_____

_____

_____

## Day 22:

### God's Divine Guidance and Intervention!
### Scripture: Psalm 32:8

**Reflection**: Either God did it or allowed it, contemplate on God's promise to guide and instruct you through it and to it.

**Prayer Prompt:** Pray for God's divine guidance and intervention in all decisions and actions.

**Questions**:

How does seeking God's guidance make you unstoppable in your purpose?

_____

_____

_____

_____

What decisions do you need God's guidance and intervention for to remain unshakeable?

_____

_____

_____

_____

How has God's guidance previously directed you toward success and security?

_____

_____

_____

_____

What practices can help you continually seek and follow God's guidance?

_____

_____

_____

_____

# Day 23:

## Overcoming Doubt and Debt!
## Scripture: Mark 11:23

**Reflection**: Reflect on the power of faith to move mountains.

**Prayer Prompt**: Pray for the removal of doubt and debt. Ask God to strengthen your faith.

**Questions:**

How can overcoming doubt and debt make you unshakeable in your faith pursuits?

_____

_____

_____

_____

What doubts and debts are currently holding you back from achieving unstoppable goals?

_____

_____

_____

_____

How has faith allowed you to overcome significant challenges in the past?

_____

_____

_____

_____

What daily practices can help you strengthen and maintain a doubt and debt-free faith?

_____

_____

_____

_____

# Day 24:

## Joy in the Lord!
**Scripture**: Nehemiah 8:10

**Reflection**: Consider the joy of the Lord as your strength.

**Prayer Prompt**: Pray for an overflowing joy in your relationship with God.

**Questions**:

How can the joy of the Lord make you unshakeable in difficult circumstances?

_____

_____

_____

_____

What sources of joy can you draw from to remain unstoppable in your endeavors?

_____

_____

_____

_____

How has the joy of the Lord been a source of strength in the past?

_____

_____

_____

_____

What actions can you take to nurture and spread joy within your community?

_____

_____

_____

_____

## Day 25:

### Embracing God's Path!
**Scripture:** 2 Corinthians 1:20

**Reflection**: Reflect on the faithfulness of God's path for your life.

**Prayer Prompt:** Pray to embrace and stand firm on God's path for your life.

**Questions**:

How can standing firm on God's path make your faith unshakeable?

_____

_____

_____

_____

What path of God have helped you become unstoppable in your journey?

_____

_____

_____

_____

How have God's path provided stability and reassurance in your life?

_____

_____

_____

What path can you take to remind yourself daily of God's faithfulness?

_____

_____

_____

_____

## Day 26:

### Word in Action!
**Scripture**: James 2:17

**Reflection**: Reflect on the importance of living out your faith.

**Prayer Prompt:** Pray for opportunities to demonstrate God's word through your actions.

**Questions**:

How does putting God's word into action make you an unstoppable witness for Christ?

_____

_____

_____

_____

What needs in your community can you address to live out God's word actively?

_____

_____

_____

_____

How has acting on God's word brought about significant changes in your life and others'?

_____

_____

_____

_____

What plans can you make to put God's word into action this week?

_____

_____

_____

_____

## Day 27:

### Unshakeable Promises!
**Scripture**: Isaiah 26:3

**Reflection**: Meditate on the perfect peace God promises.

**Prayer Prompt**: Pray for unshakeable peace in every aspect of your life.

**Questions**:

How can cultivating unshakeable peace make you unstoppable in your daily activities?

_____

_____

_____

_____

What situations or challenges currently disrupt your peace?

_____

_____

_____

_____

How has God's promises sustained you in past trials and tribulations?

_____

_____

_____

_____

What practical steps can you take to maintain peace amidst chaos and conflict?

_____

_____

_____

_____

## Day 28:

### God's Invisible Hand!
**Scripture:** Hebrews 13:8

**Reflection**: Reflect on the unchanging nature of Jesus Christ.

**Prayer Prompt:** Pray for trust in God's invisible hand.

**Questions**:

How does knowing God's unchanging nature help you remain unshakeable in faith?

_____

_____

_____

_____

In what ways does God's invisible hand empower you to be unstoppable?

_____

_____

_____

_____

How has God's invisible hand provided comfort and stability in your life?

_____

_____

_____

_____

What daily practices can help you rely more on God's invisible hand?

_____

_____

_____

_____

## Day 29:

### Resilience in Faith!
**Scripture**: 2 Corinthians 4:8-9

**Reflection**: Consider how God sustains you through every hardship.

**Prayer Prompt:** Pray for resilience and unwavering faith.

**Questions:**

How does resilience in your faith make you unbreakable in challenging times?

_____

_____

_____

_____

What hardships are you facing that require divine resilience?

_____

_____

_____

_____

How has resilience in faith made you unstoppable in achieving your goals?

_____

_____

_____

_____

What steps can you take to build and sustain resilience in your daily walk with God?

_____

_____

_____

_____

## Day 30:

### Hope Again!
**Scripture:** Psalm 119:105

**Reflection**: Reflect on the guidance and hope found in God's Word.

**Prayer Prompt:** Pray for a deeper love and understanding of the Bible.

**Questions:**

How does the guidance from God's Word make you unshakeable in your hope?

_____

_____

_____

_____

What specific scriptures provide hope and help you remain unstoppable in faith?

_____

_____

_____

_____

How has God's Word been a light in the dark times of despair?

_____

_____

_____

_____

What actions can you take to immerse yourself more deeply in the Bible?

_____

_____

_____

_____

## Day 31:

### Living Unstoppable, Unbreakable, Unshakeable!
**Scripture**: Philippians 4:13

**Reflection**: Embrace the strength of actively living through Christ.

**Prayer Prompt:** Thank God for making you unstoppable, unbreakable, and unshakeable in Him. Ask for continued revelational growth and faithfulness.

**Questions:**

How has this 31-day journey inspired you to be unstoppable in your everyday life?

_____

_____

_____

_____

In what ways have you become unbreakable through your faith and experiences?

_____

_____

_____

_____

How will building unshakeable faith make a difference in your generation and future generations to come?

_____

_____

_____

_____

What commitments will you make to ensure the next generations continue growing in these areas?

_____

_____

_____

_____

SCAN FOR MORE BOOKS :

Send Testimonials:
Email: RichPSuccessful@gmail.com

published by IAmEncouragement, LLC